Influencing Organizational Culture

Stefan Kühl is professor of sociology at the University of Bielefeld in Germany and works as a consultant for Metaplan, a consulting firm based in Princeton, Hamburg, Shanghai, Singapore, Versailles and Zurich. He studied sociology and history at the University of Bielefeld (Germany), Johns Hopkins University in Baltimore (USA), Université Paris-X-Nanterre (France) and the University of Oxford (UK).

Other Books by Stefan Kühl

Organizations: A Systems Approach
(Routledge 2013)
Ordinary Organizations: Why Normal Men Carried Out the Holocaust
(Polity Press 2016)
When the Monkeys Run the Zoo: The Pitfalls of Flat Hierarchies
(Organizational Dialogue Press 2017)
Sisyphus in Management: The Futile Search for the Optimal Organizational Structure
(Organizational Dialogue Press 2018)
The Rainmaker Effect: Contradictions of the Learning Organization
(Organizational Dialogue Press 2018)

To contact us:
Metaplan
101 Wall Street
Princeton, NJ 08540
USA
Phone: +1 609-688-9171
stefankuehl@metaplan.com
www.metaplan.com

Stefan Kühl

Influencing Organizational Culture

A Very Brief Introduction

Organizational Dialogue Press
Princeton, Hamburg, Shanghai, Singapore, Versailles, Zurich

ISBN (Print) 978-1-7323861-4-3
ISBN (EPUB) 978-1-7323861-5-0

Copyright © 2018 by Stefan Kühl

All rights reserved. No part of this publication may be reproduced or transmitted in any form or by any means, without permission in writing from the author.

Translated by: Lee Holt
Cover Design: Guido Klütsch
Typesetting: Thomas Auer
Project Management: Tabea Koepp
www.organizationaldialoguepress.com

Contents

Preface 7

1.
Organizational Culture—What Is It About? 12

1.1. The Culture of Organizations—
The Undecided Decision Premise 12
1.2. Types of Organizational Cultural Expectations 19
1.3. The Three Sides of Organizations 25

2.
The Temptations and Limits of an
Instrumental-Rational Approach 29

2.1. The Reactivation of an Old Hope for Control 30
2.2. Characteristics of a "Malleable" Organizational Culture 33
2.3. The Failure of Cultural Programs 37

3.
Leverage for Influencing Organizational Culture 46

    3.1. Formalization of Programs, Communication Channels
        and Personnel as Leverage...49

    3.2. Abandonment of Formalization as a Strategy for
        Changing Organizational Culture...52

    3.3. Increased Formalization as a Starting Point for
        Shaping the Organizational Culture......................................56

4.
Conclusion—Consequences for Influencing
Organizational Cultures 60

Bibliography..68

Preface

Whenever a problem is identified in a company, an administration, a hospital, a school or a university, blame for the it is typically assigned to the organization's culture. Then the talk is about a "culture of fear" that has led to important information not being passed up the chain of command. A diagnosis is delivered of a "culture of wants" consisting of an orientation towards results, self-motivation, enthusiasm and job satisfaction, in which all employees may be in a permanent flow, yet can no longer perceive their own limits. Or we find a "culture of victims" in which the organization appears as a vale of tears from which no escape seems possible.

These kinds of short descriptions of cultures may prove persuasive due to their concise catchiness, but in analytical terms they merely scratch the surface of the organization. The short formula of the "culture of fear" casts a shadow over how such fears crept into the organization in the first place, where exactly in the organization fear is being produced, and what effects result from it for example on the willingness to deviate from the rules when it's needed. The "culture of wants" has a positive touch, but it leaves open where these desires emanate from and what the exact costs are of such inclinations. The "culture of victims" meme has a certain amount of traction, but by its nature it undermines a deeper analysis of cultural expectations towards behavior.

The aim of this book is to enable readers to identify, in a precise and comprehensive way, an organization's culture, and to articulate starting points for changing it. This is why it is necessary to liberate discussions about organizational cultures from the humanist and harmony-seeking ballast that has crept into the target definitions of cultures in organizations. Of course, it is understandable when managers and consultants prefer a culture of trust or distrust, or find an innovation-oriented culture better than a bureaucratic one. But in the end, the talk on values, ubiquitous in management and consulting discourse, obscures an accurate view of the organization.

Organizational culture is usually defined too broadly, incorporating such phenomena as assumptions, values, traditions, articles of faith, myths and artifacts; we want to work with a narrower, more precisely articulated definition. Our understanding of organizational culture is shaped by the theory of social systems. From this perspective, an organizational culture is comprised of expectations of the behavior of the organization's members. In the case of culture those expectations have not been made through officials by management but instead emerge slowly, through repetitions and imitations. This more precise definition allows us to mark off organizational culture (or we could call it the informal structure) against two things: first, against the formal structure, and second, against the organization's display side, which was created for presenting the organization to the outside world (Chapter 1). This definition helps to avoid an error that has seeped into the debate among practitioners in management and in consulting. This error is based on the notion that an analysis of current organizational culture must be followed by the definition of a target culture that can then be attained by the implementation of various cultural measures by management (Chapter 2). We believe that this idea of organizational culture is an expression of the exaggerated illusions of control held by managers and consultants, and that it tends to contribute to the obfuscation of the organizational culture that actually exists. It may sound like a paradox, but the only way to influence an organization's culture (its informal structure) is to change the formal structure (Chapter 3). Instead of following standard practice and drawing a distinction between changing the formal structure and projects for changing organizational culture, we argue in the conclusion for the idea that cultural projects only make sense if there is an opportunity to begin with changing the formal structure (Chapter 4).

The approach we present here for working on organizational cultures is based on our several years of experiences in working with companies, ministries, administrations, armed forces, police forces, universities, schools, hospitals and non-profit organizations. Even if this book has emerged out of practical work, we still believe that our approach resonates with insights from scholarly organization theory.

We believe that organization theoreticians and practitioners in organizations have fundamentally different quality criteria. The assumption that "good science" necessarily leads to "good practice" is naive because the criteria that scientists use to define success differ fundamentally from those of practitioners. Yet despite this difference, which we believe is insuperable, our aspiration here is to present a proven approach in such a way that organization theorists cannot dismiss it right away as uninteresting. And even if this slim volume is written primarily for practitioners, attentive organization theorists may also discover some interesting theoretical innovations in it.

This book is part of the *Management Compact* series in which we present the essentials for the management of organizations against the background of modern organizational theories. In addition to this volume, *Influencing Organizational Culture*, the series includes books on the subjects of *Developing Strategies*, *Managing Projects*, *Designing Organizations*, *Developing Mission Statements*, and *Exploring Markets*. In our book on *Lateral Leading*, we assess how power, understanding and trust influence the management of organizations. Because these books are all based on the same understanding of organizations, attentive readers will notice related trains of thought and similar formulations across the volumes in this series. These overlaps were created intentionally to emphasize the unity of the ideas behind the series and to highlight the connections in between.

You can read more about the theoretical foundations behind this concept in *Organizations: A Systems Approach* (Kühl 2013); the first chapter of this book in particular builds on these foundations, presenting the advantages of a narrow understanding of organizational culture. Those interested in empirical evaluations of organizational cultures that apply the distinctions introduced in this book may be referred to *Sisyphus in Management: The Futile Search for the Optimal Organizational Structure* (Kühl 2018, forthcoming). And for readers interested in how this concept can be used for the historical analysis of organizations, we recommend *Ordinary Organizations: Why Normal Men Carried out the Holocaust* (Kühl 2016).

We do not believe in texts that demand too little from managers and consultants by crowding our texts with bullet points, executive summaries, or exercises. The *Management Compact* series presents brief books that enable readers to understand the central ideas without these kinds of aids. Along with a very limited number of graphics, there is only one element that makes reading easier: small boxes. We use these to present examples that illustrate our ideas, or to mark productive connections to organization theory. Readers who are short on time or are not interested in these aspects can skip over the text boxes without losing the thread.

This book was developed in the Metaplan training program, "Management and Consulting in Discourse." We would like to thank the participants in the various cohorts with which we tried out and refined *Influencing Organizational Culture* for their many tips and ideas.

1. Organizational Culture—What Is It About?

In management discourse, hardly any term is thrown about more carelessly and with less accuracy than organizational culture. Organizational culture is understood as the "fundamental assumptions," "taken-for-granted behavior" and "values presented to the outside world," as well as "artifacts" such as architecture, furniture and clothing (Schein 1985, 12). Some believe that organizational culture is the "totality of norms and values" that constitute the "spirit and personality" of an organization (Doppler/Lauterburg 2002, 451). Organizational culture includes such varied phenomena as cognitive abilities (Schnyder 1992, 63), mindsets (Kobi/Wüthrich 1986, 13), the climate of an organization (Schein 1985, 21) or attained patterns or knowledge (Klimecki et al. 1994, 80). Organizational culture is "described as a collection of traditions, values, strategies, articles of faith, and sets of attitudes" (Marshall/Mclean 1985, 2ff.), or—to put it in a more complicated way—as "self-referential contexts of meaning" in an organization (Bardmann/Franzpötter 1990, 434). Organizational culture also summarizes the myths, stories and legends that circulate within an organization (Frost et al. 1985, 17), as well as the heroes that shape an organization's style (Rodríguez Mansilla 2004, 57).

The idea of organizational culture seems to serve as a "terminological vacuum cleaner" that sucks up everything that has something to do with organizations. Values, norms, business models, rules, symbols, ways of thinking, sets of beliefs, myths, dogma, meanings—everything is summed up in the notion of organizational culture and mixed up. The concept of organizational culture is therefore threatened by the same fate that has befallen other ideas about management or strategy that are used too expansively in management discourse: conceptual arbitrariness. The consequence here is that a broadly defined notion of organizational culture often captures the same empirical phenomena and normative recommendations as the terms of leadership or strategy. Consequently, the idea of a "mindset" among members of an organization is being discussed under the term of organizational culture as under the term of strategy. Or discussions about behaviors or attitudes take place under the aegis of leadership or a broad idea of organizational culture (Alvesson 2013, 83/99f.; Kühl 2017).

To be sure, the expansive, almost arbitrary usage of the term organizational culture—much like the uncontrolled use of terms such as leadership or strategy—creates the foundation for successful communication with and among practitioners. These terms, when they are defined as ambiguously, suggest connectivity because almost any phenomenon in an organization can be associated with these concepts; at the same time, they unleash positive associations because they promise possibilities for intervention into the organization. However, this terminological ambiguity obscures what is actually at issue. According to a widespread complaint, this lack of precision in the discussion about organizational culture that has been lead over decades has led to a lack of clarity about fundamental concepts, such as "what culture is," "what features a culture has," "what it comprises," "what effects it has," or "how it should be examined" (Sackmann 1991, 8f.).

From the perspective of organizational studies, however, it is not at all difficult to define this term in a precise way. "Organizational culture" means all of the behavioral expectations that have slowly crept in over time and have not been established by means of decisions. Organizational theory describes organizational culture as those decision premises in organizations about which no decisions have been made (Rodríguez Mansilla 1991, 140f.). Practitioners may find this definition irritating at first. Decision premises: what's that supposed to mean? And what in the world are decision premises about which no decisions have been made? We admit that this definition of organizational culture may seem complicated at first glance. If we take a closer look, though, it's actually quite simple. We need only examine how cultural expectations within the organization—the undecided decision premises—form and develop.

1.1 The Culture of Organizations— The Undecided Decision Premise

In order to better understand this concept, let's start with the banal observation that people develop expectations in order to be able to get along with each other. We know that you are supposed to say hello when you knock at a stranger's door and the stranger opens the door (Goffman 1967, 55f.). We know how to behave when waiting in a line, and we get in trouble if we don't follow these rules (Mann 1969, 342ff.). If we were unable to rely on these social expectations, which we could also call social structures, then life would be very complicated, if not impossible.

Expectations serve as points of reference for specific actions, yet they do not determine how people act. Even if you know that you're supposed to say hello when a stranger opens their door to you, you can choose not to greet them. But then you have to be prepared for people to think you're a weirdo. You can try to push your way to the front of a line. But you'll probably be on the receiving end of angry stares, clear verbal reprimands, or even a little shove, all of which tell you that you've violated the expectations about how to conduct yourself in a waiting line. Expectations therefore do not have the function of "precisely sketching out specific actions;" instead, they supply the "room for de facto behavior" (Luhmann 1964, 272). In brief, you can deviate from social expectations, but then you have to bear the consequences.

When defining organizational culture, it is important to understand that expectations develop in two different ways: expectations are either decided on by management, legislation or the head of a family; or expectations creep in through imitation and repetition, without any clear decisions being made about them (Young 1989, 201). To take a simple example, in American football, there are both the "written rules" laid down in the NFL rulebooks as well as the "unwritten rules." For example, there is an expectation that, if a player on the opposing team is injured on the field, that a team will somehow stop the clock to allow the player to receive treatment. This is an expectation that stems not from a decision by the NFL, but rather from practices that have proven themselves and thereby became standard.

We can illustrate the difference with the following example. When designing a park, the city administration makes decisions about where the paths should be set up. The course of these paths creates expectations about where park visitors can go. Yet beaten paths appear very quickly. No one made any decisions about these vernacular paths, but they arise from repeated use. Once the beaten paths are really stamped down, the expectation that these beaten paths can be used is similar to the expectation that the "official" paths laid down by the city administration should be used.

THEORY

In systems theory, a social structure is understood as expectations to which behavior must be oriented (Luhmann 1984, 398). "All contacts between people" are, according to Niklas Luhmann, "controlled by complementary behavioral expectations." "You have to act within the channels mapped out and made acceptable by expectations"; otherwise, "you are misunderstood and rejected" (Luhmann 1964, 272). Certain expectations are then "compiled into systems" as behavioral premises, for example in organizations, protest movements, families or groups of friends, thereby stabilizing these expectations in a "relatively disappointment-proof way" (Luhmann 1972, 31).

In the course of these developments, specific expectations form within the different social systems. You don't have to have

> a Ph.D. to know that protest movements and families have different expectations of behavior, or that expectations differ between organizations and groups of friends. If you were to ignore this and as a retired business man tried to run your family like a business, then your spouse and children would probably tell you that you are acting strange. There are certainly cases where these different social systems overlap; we need to only think of organizations that emerge from protest movements, or groups of friends who found a start-up company together, or a family business. Yet we can see quite clearly in these social systems how there is a constant balancing act about which system logics are currently in force.

In many social situations, expectations develop without much being decided. Lovestruck couples typically don't sign a contract governing social interactions before they enter a relationship. Ways of interacting on a daily basis, dividing up tasks in the household, and sexual practices creep in as expectations, and later on prove to be very difficult to change. In the same way, parent-child relationships are shaped very little by decisions. Although parents again and again try to introduce firm rules for living together, actual behavior expectations develop through the often spontaneous toleration or rejection of specific actions by each other.

In comparison to lovers or families, however, there are social entities that are very decisive: organizations. Organizations are constantly making decisions with which members have to comply if they want to remain members. Management specifies the period of time that someone has to be present in the organization's offices, what someone has to do while they are there, which other organization members deserve attention and who can be ignored. These decided membership conditions constitute an organization's *formal structure*. We can also express this in a more complicated way by calling these conditions the fixed or decided decision premises of an organization.

At the same time, however, organizations develop in subtle ways an *informal structure*—the organizational culture. This revolves around specifications that do not emerge through decisions made by executive boards, political party congresses or the Pope; they have emerged as habits and have become successfully established. Informal structures thus are not the nonrecurring improvisations that blaze a trail through a thicket of rules and regulations; instead, they are the network of proven beaten paths that are being traversed again and again in an organization. It is only when coordination with a colleague in a neighboring department ceases to be an exception and becomes a recurring "shortcut" for coordination that we are looking at an organization's cultural expectations, its undecided decision premises (Rodríguez Mansilla 1991, 140f.).

There are various reasons why cultural expectations develop in organizations. Not all expectations in organizations are elevated to the status of membership conditions. It is precisely when we are dealing with attitudes and styles of thinking that it becomes difficult, if not impossible, to translate them into such things as membership conditions. Just take a look at the desperate attempts by consultants and HR development when they try to teach their clients creativity, spontaneity or authenticity. The subtle influence exercised by informal expectations—the organizational culture—plays a central role here. In organizational sciences, we call these *undecidable decision premises* (Kühl 2013, 120). However, there are also expectations that can in principle be formalized, and compliance could be monitored, yet organizations decide, whether consciously or unconsciously, to forego their formalization. In organizational sciences, we call these *decision premises that are decidable although they have not been decided on* (Kühl 2013, 120). The development of these premises has to do with the fact that organizations are confronted with contradictory demands that cannot be met by decision-making at the formal level. According to an early observation by Niklas Luhmann, there can always only be *one* "consistently planned, legitimate, formal order of expectations" in organizations (Luhmann 1964, 155). Because organizations have to react to contradictory demands, yet simultaneously pay attention to the fact that their members are confronted with a consistent and therefore largely contradiction-free formal structure, nothing else remains for them to do aside from tolerating—or even supporting—informality, perhaps even illegality (Luhmann 1964, 86).

1.2 Types of Organizational Cultural Expectations

Expectations in organizations develop in the form of three types of structure. *Programs* bundle criteria according to which decisions are made. Programs include for example managerial target systems, work instructions, IT programs and policies. They are used to determine what kind of behavior in organizations is to be viewed as right or wrong. *Communication channels* describe how and in what ways people can, or must, communicate within an organization. A small number of legitimate contacts are permitted via communication channels, and members have to comply with these contact restrictions unless they want to put their membership at risk. *Personnel* is the third type of expectation formation in organizations. It makes a difference for future decisions which people or what kind of person are put into a position. At the same time the decision premise of personnel can be influenced for example by hiring, relocations or HR development. All three types of expectation formation display both formal and informal manifestations.

An organization uses *programs*, the first basic type of structure, to determine the conditions under which decisions can be accepted as right. The orientation towards formal programs is raised up to the level of a membership requirement. It is impossible to remain in the organization if you openly reject these programs. One option for the formal "programming of an organization" is to set up conditional programs, which include work processes and workflows in organizations and in IT systems. These are if-then programs that determine precisely how to react to a specific input. A second option is to define goal programs in the form of business objective systems, strategic aims or target agreements. These programs set down which objectives are supposed to be attained; the selection of the means to obtain these ends, however, remains largely open (regarding the difference, see Luhmann 2000, 263ff.).

The formal programming of organizations, however, is not without risk. The first problem is that formal programs are inevitably not always appropriate for specific situations. It is clearly not possible to anticipate every situation and develop special rules for dealing with it. This is why strict adherence to programs can threaten to block organizations. Just try, for one entire working day, to clarify all of the relevant rules and then slavishly follow them. During this little experiment, you would see rising frustration among colleagues about this exaggerated "formalist behavior." The second problem is that formally defined programs exercise a significant influence on how organizations perceive their environment. This is backed up by an idea that has become largely accepted in organizational research, namely that an organization's structure shapes its perception of the exterior world (Weick 1995). An organization's programs function like filters that only let compatible information through. This reinforces the organization's belief that their current organizational structure is the right one, and its programs, which seem to prove themselves, are further consolidated and refined. This creates a real circle of self-affirmation in which organizations receive constant confirmation of their functioning, due to how they perceive their environment through their own filters.

For these reasons, it makes functional sense that organizations develop informal programs alongside their formal programs. Informal conditional programs are routines about which no decisions were ever made at a central level; for example, the trick of clocking out at the end of a working day, and then to continue working, so that you don't violate regulatory or company limits on working hours; precisely arranged dealings with slush funds in organizations; or the illegally practiced obligation of MPs in many parties to pay parts of their diets to their parties. Informal goal programs revolve around goals that are not formulated as a formal expectation. These programs are the processing of orders for a few special customers who receive preferential treatment despite all rules set, or the secret development of microchips, medications or even entire cars, without ever having an official assignment from top management.

Organizations make decisions about *communication channels*, the second basic structural type, in that they define hierarchies, signatory powers, and project structures. By setting up formal communication channels, the possibilities for communication in the organization are substantially restricted. Only a small number of legitimate communication channels are permitted, and members have to use them unless they want to put their membership at risk. Every organization therefore limits, first of all, a "basic condition of human possibilities," namely that "anyone can communicate with anyone, anytime, about anything" (Luhmann 1970, 7).

Organizations, however, cannot rely on their formal communication channels alone, because not every need for communication can be satisfied in these channels. Let's just imagine for a moment what would happen if all of an organization's members were to strictly follow the formally prescribed channels for communication and decision-making. The heads of organizations would only be informed by their direct reports about relevant events; in hierarchical communication, hierarchic intermediaries could not be bypassed, and coordination across departmental boundaries could only be made by the positions responsible for them, which are typically concentrated at the top of the organization. The result would be an enormous slowdown in communication and decision-making processes that would, in the final analysis, pose an existential threat to the organization.

This is why informal communication channels necessarily develop in every organization. In organizations with departments set up according to functional, regional or customer-specific aspects, we often find informal communication shortcuts alongside formally prescribed communication channels that enable quick coordination across departmental boundaries. In organizations with multiple levels of hierarchy, there is a tendency to accelerate coordination processes by jumping over direct supervisors to reach agreement directly with the next-higher superior. In organizations with comparatively few levels of hierarchy, pronounced informal leaders often emerge who make it possible to quickly reach an agreement, between people at the same level of hierarchy, about a joint approach.

When we talk about *personnel*, the third basic type of structure in organizations, we are talking about structures that, as HR decisions, are an important lever for how decisions are made. After all, when it comes to an organization's future decisions, it makes a difference who occupies a position. There are various formal options for organizations when it comes to fine-tuning human resources: hiring, firing, internal transfers and HR development (Luhmann 1971, 208). Formal job profiles are defined for positions, economic or legal criteria for dismissals, official career paths are set up, or HR development measures are developed that are binding for all employees. By doing this, an organization limits their own options for recruitment and reallocation of personnel, but manages to create a foundation for integrating thousands or tens of thousands of people into an organization.

Often there are only limited options for getting an organization in a position to fill all positions with the "right personnel" if only the formal structures are referred to. Organizations would unavoidably make suboptimal staffing decisions if they went about recruiting personnel solely on the base of the formal demands made by the human resources department and the staff council. The training of new employees would be insufficient if it only included formal educational efforts by the HR department. Hierarchical staff relocations would not always lead to hiring a person who fits the job profile if they were oriented entirely to the career paths strictly prescribed by the HR division.

This is why informal decision-making processes also develop in the field of personnel. In addition to the official conditions for posting a position, when filling a position, those doing the hiring often attend to criteria that are not formally specified, such as social adaptability, personal contact networks, membership in a trade union, or political affinities. The official career paths are supplemented by unofficial career paths that allow individuals to be raised to the formal standards set by the human resources department. Informal socialization in the work process by colleagues is more important for adapting personnel to the demands of the organization than education through formally defined HR development measures. And in the case of dismissals, in addition to the official criteria that can be made plausible before labor courts, unofficial criteria that cannot be openly addressed are often used.

1.3 The Three Sides of Organizations

In order to better understand the culture of an organization, we have to systematically distinguish between the three sides of an organization (Kühl 2013, 88ff.). The *formal side* is about the official body of rules to which members have to feel bound. These are the membership conditions that someone has to fulfill if they want to remain a member. The *informal (organizational cultural) side* of an organization consists of long-established practices, of neat tricks to make work easier, and of regular deviations from formal rules. The *display side* is the facade of an organization. It is meant to present something by means of its embellishments, ornamentation, or perhaps its evenness (Rottenburg 1996, 191ff.). Organizations present the most attractive facade possible to the outside world so that they can attract customer favor, influence the media to attain the best possible coverage, or to receive legitimation by politics.

If we want to describe organizations with the unavoidably simplifying metaphor of the human body, (on organization metaphors in general, see Morgan 1986), then they consist not only of a skeleton (the formal structure) but also of a nervous system (the informal structure) and a skin: a structure that represents the display side, but also protects the body against the environment (Krackhardt/Hanson 1993). The skeleton does not display itself immediately, but can be rendered easily visible with appropriate aids. The nervous system, on the other hand, is difficult to recognize, even if it is crucial for the existence of the human body. The skin is what you immediately recognize when you look at a body, which is why people dress it up with make-up or tattoos.

Only if you systematically keep an eye on the three sides of the organization can you avoid two fundamental mistakes that are frequently made in the discussion about organizational cultures. The first mistake is that the informal (organizational cultural) side of the organization is not related systematically enough to the formal side. Even if informal programs, communication channels and decisions on personnel are identified in detail within the framework of a cultural analysis, they are not always related to formal programs, communication channels and personnel decisions. There is a dominant idea that one can understand an organizational-cultural structure without having to grasp in detail how it is shaped by the formal structure, what gaps in the formal structure it fills and where it comes into conflict with the formal structure. The second mistake is that in the discussion on organizational cultures there is no fundamental distinction between the informal (organizational cultural) side and the display side of the organization. The idea is that the values presented to the outside world, such as innovative ability, competitiveness and the ability to deal with conflicts, can largely be brought into line with the organizational norms of action dominating the informal side. What is overlooked, however, is that the function of the display side, which is so important for the production of legitimacy, is completely different from that of the informal side, which is more concerned with the very important formation of organizational-cultural expectations of behavior adapted to everyday problems.

Certainly, depending on the project, focus shifts to different sides of the organization. Whereas classic reorganization projects are usually concerned with changing the formal side of the orga-

Organizational Culture—What Is It About? **27**

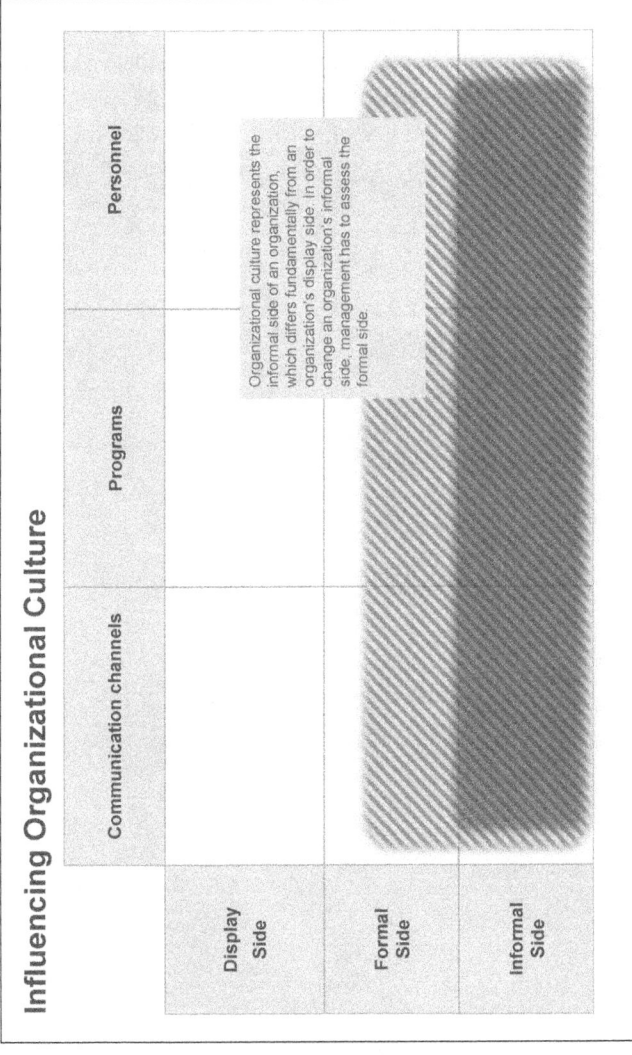

Diagram 1: Structural Matrix for Analyzing Organizations

nization and, in the creation of a mission statement, primarily with reworking the display side, the informal side is the focal point of projects that focus on the organizational culture. The challenge is to keep an eye on all three sides with their very different functions.

2. The Temptations and Limits of an Instrumental-Rational Approach

Organizational culture is malleable: this is the credo of the management literature on organizational culture. The aim is to use "meaning-transporting measures" to make employees aware of their organization's "mission." Employees are to be involved in the development of a cultural mission statement in order to reflect together on changes in the organization's culture. The "incentive systems" should be designed in such a way that values such as "customer orientation," "collegiality," "willingness to innovate," "quality awareness," "conflict management" and "sense of community" are promoted at the same time. An internal "rotation of bearers of subculture" should contribute to the "promotion of internal knowledge and acceptance of the subcultural structure." "Interdisciplinary learning group compositions" shall serve as a "measure of HR development" in order to anchor the organization's propagated values in the organizational culture (Bleicher 1986, 105). Imagination seems to have no limits when it comes to proposals on how to shape organizational culture.

A central role in the establishment of organizational culture is attributed to management. According to this idea, managers would shape the culture of the organization by credibly representing and exemplifying its values. They would be able to exercise a direct influence on the organizational culture through the questions they ask their employees, the topics they talk about with them, and the issues that are important to them. According to the management literature, it makes sense for managers to rotate between the different areas of the organization in order to establish a uniform culture within the organization. "Managers without portfolios"—"culture evangelists"—could also be appointed to raise questions, critically question convictions and propose new ideas (Lorsch 1986, 105).

It is being demanded that organizations define their own culture through "culture audits" (see for example Solomon 2004) or "cultural due diligences" (Carleton/Lineberry 2010)—especially in comparison to the cultures of other organizations. It is important that all members of the organization, with all their strengths and weaknesses, come to an agreement about the prevailing organizational culture. Writing down the results of these "cultural audits" and "cultural due diligences" would make it clear to everyone what basic cultural beliefs prevail in the organization, and it would be possible to identify where cultural change is needed. It is hoped that, through this confrontation with themselves, organizations will be ready for a fundamental change of culture.

2.1 The Reactivation of an Old Hope for Control

The approach to shaping the organizational culture is ultimately the reactivation of an old control fantasy: management's dream of designing the informal networks, the hidden incentive structures and implicit thought patterns in the organization in such a way that they make the organization more successful. The "human relations approach," which became popular before the Second World War, was already dominated by the idea that organizations become a haven of humanity and economic excellence if only the informal structure can be designed accordingly. People felt that the various existing negotiations, implicit coordination, ad hoc agreements, etc. could be controlled by management in a way that ultimately everyone would benefit (Roethlisberger/Dickson 1939; Mayo 1948).

As was the case with other management modalities, the idea that the success of organizations is based on informal networks, implicit norms and the basic attitudes of employees was reactivated every fifteen or twenty years. In the mid-1950s, the idea that the "spirit of organization" plays a central role in the success of an organization became more and more accepted in the ranks of management (Drucker 1954). Following Abraham Maslow's hierarchy of needs (Maslow 1954), it was emphasized that the satisfaction of basic needs such as eating, drinking and sleeping are not the only important thing to human beings, but needs for security, recognition, appreciation and self-realization also play an important role. The working climate and the working conditions became increasingly important.

In the 1980s, "soft aspects" were once again discovered as formative success factors in the "search for excellence" in the field of organizational culture (Peters/Waterman 1982; Deal/Kennedy 1982). The success of Japanese companies had destroyed the management myth shaped by the USA, and the organizational culture of Asian companies was identified as a strategic advantage. However, instead of explaining the success of Asian organizations by recognizing their embeddedness in their cultural traditions, which is not the case with American and European organizations, emphasis was placed on the possibility of each individual company to shape its own organizational culture (Ouchi 1981). The "corporate culture" boom covered both practitioners and application-oriented researchers who used scientific vocabulary to buttress management's hopes for the shaping of organizational culture (Schein 1985; Schein 1999; Schein 1996).

During the New Economy wave in the late 1990s, this body of ideas experienced a renaissance in the culture of start-up companies. Consultants rated organizational culture as a success factor not only for small face-to-face organizations but also for large companies. Organizations established positions such as "Chief Culture Officer," "Chief Happiness Officer," "Director of People and Culture" or "Feel-Good Manager." Praise was heaped upon Enron or WorldCom as cultural models shortly before they went bankrupt and their board members were imprisoned (see for example the book by the McKinsey consultants Foster/Kaplan 2001). Yet despite the spectacular failure of some pioneering organizations in the field of culture, the idea that "culture matters" was successfully reactivated.

The topic of organizational culture gained renewed momentum with the popularity of approaches on New Work in the beginning of the 2010s. In the slipstream of management fashions such as agility and holacracy, which once again propagated the principles of de-formalization, breakdown of hierarchies and decentralization, the topic of culture also gained renewed importance. Because executives would lose their potential influence through the dismantling of hierarchies and the decentralization of competencies, it was argued that it was all the more important to provide them with another instrument for controlling the organization by shaping the corporate culture.

The cyclically recurring popularity of organizational culture among managers can be explained as a reaction to perceived problems of control. With the concept of organizational culture, managers can on the one hand renounce the classical concepts of control, but on the other hand maintain the idea of controlling organizational order, even if it is more difficult to execute (Luhmann 2000, 239f.). Because the organizational culture enables a "collective programming of the mind" (Hofstede 1980, 13), it was possible, according to management thought, to align their organizations by means of decentralization, even in the case of centrifugal forces. Because the "hearts, souls and minds" of organizations could be managed through organizational culture (Deetz et al. 2000, 1), managers no longer had to hold organizations together by means of hierarchical commands and precise programs (Gagliardi 1986, 117ff.). At the end of the day—so runs the idea in management—there is "no more efficient means of management than a distinctive, coherent organizational culture" (Doppler/Lauterberg 2002, 452).

2.2 Characteristics of a "Malleable" Organizational Culture

If we read reports and presentations on projects to change organizational cultures in companies, administrations, hospitals or schools, they are characterized by a high degree of consistency, coherence and rationality. Regardless of whether it is the introduction of new guiding principles for cooperation between departments, the establishment of a quality culture or the development of a common organizational culture after a merger: the success stories are usually dominated by the description of rationally planned reorganizations. Although obstacles, resistances, uncertainties and unforeseen events are reported, these problems are usually successfully overcome by those in charge of culture through a sudden idea, a newly developed instrument for cultural change, or a daring intervention at a cultural change conference. Presentations promise a well-planned and flexible process with which participants can change their culture in an intentional way.

This kind of understanding of culture usually serves to idealize the target culture. The description of the organizational culture to which an organization aspires is loaded with positive values (Alvesson 2013, 202). The organization's culture is said to include such important values as "customer focus," "employee satisfaction," "quality awareness," "responsibility for results," "willingness to innovate," "open communication," "collegial work styles," "readiness to manage conflict" and "a feeling of community." People assume that the various positive values are all complementary to each other. A high level of "employee satisfaction" is thought to lead to improved "collegiality," which results in "improved conflict resolution," increases the "willingness to innovate" and improves the "customer focus," which then increases "employee satisfaction." In accordance with the idea that "all good things go together" (Huntington 1968, 4), all of the good values in an organization would not only complement but even mutually reinforce one another.

What is striking here is the standardization of the target culture (Alvesson 2013, 202). The idea is that the identification of all organization members with the same values and the resulting "strong organizational culture" contribute significantly to the success of an organization (on this approach, see the examples from innumerable similar works such as Sackmann 2006; Taylor 2015; Connors/Smith 2012). This does not necessarily mean a harmonious understanding of culture. It is indeed admitted that there are different subcultures within an organization. "Diversity" has become such a widely accepted value that even in organizations characterized by white, male and elderly people, it is important to ensure that publicly used photos show a diverse mix of age groups, genders and ethnic origins in order to suggest organizational diversity, according to the motto: It is this diversity that forms the common denominator of the organization.

Another characteristic is the emphasis of the uniqueness of one's own organizational culture. This may go hand in hand with the management literature's preference of the concept of organizational culture over the concept of informality, which is considered to be "outdated." With the concept of culture, which originated in anthropology, the aim was to focus more strongly on the special qualities of individual "excellent companies" compared to many less excellent companies. The "other," as Mats Alvesson points out, is used as a point of comparison to highlight an organization's own peculiarity (Alvesson 2013, 203). This emphasis on uniqueness may come as a surprise, because organizations are surprisingly similar when it comes to identifying target cultures. Values such as "customer focus," "employee satisfaction," "quality awareness," "responsibility for results," "willingness to innovate," "open communication," "collegial work styles," "readiness to manage conflict" and "a feeling of community" litter the definitions of target cultures in almost every organization, from Sweden to Zimbabwe and from Chile to North Korea. In defining one's own culture, however, clear boundaries are drawn to other cultures for differentiation. Organizations contrast their own "entrepreneurial culture" with the "bureaucratic culture" of other companies or emphasize the "people-centered culture" of their own company against the "anonymous culture" of other companies. Simplified descriptions are often used, and the differences are emphasized excessively in order to make one's own culture scintillate in its uniqueness.

Ultimately, this approach to organizational culture is a simplified variant of the instrumental-rational organizational model. In the classical instrumental-rational understanding of organizations, it is still assumed that the difference between the status quo and the target image can be overcome by a machine-like construction of the organization. Organizations, like machines, would have to orient themselves towards a clearly defined purpose and align all resources to it. According to the classical instrumental-rational model, organizations are like machines, a self-contained whole comprised of precisely defined individual parts.

In the case of cultural processes, a shortcut is proposed in contrast to the classical instrumental-rational model. In processes for shaping the organizational culture, employees would work together on a "target culture" in which the forms of conflict resolution, cooperation and assumption of responsibility would be defined in order to achieve the goals of the organization. In contrast to an "as-is culture," which is characterized by cooperation difficulties, coordination conflicts and power struggles, a "target culture" is created, which satisfies the managers' longing for organizations as harmonious, finely tuned, all-encompassing pieces of art. In order to achieve this target culture, focus is consequently placed on the "soft factors:" how to design rules of cooperation between managers and employees to everyone's satisfaction? Which signals can be sent by making it possible to create a more relaxed dress code? How can joint activities such as company celebrations, singing rounds, company runs, golf tournaments and Kilimanjaro ascents strengthen cohesion? How can an improvement in coffee quality increase creativity? How can the option to bring along cats, dogs and horses to the workplace improve collegial interaction? Ultimately, the hope is that the values developed in a cultural process and supported by cultural measures would directly impact the behavior of employees, making a machine-like and precise set of rules in this area superfluous.

2.3 The Failure of Cultural Programs

In their presentation to the world organizational culture projects are generally celebrated as great successes. People act as though the great-sounding catalog of values created during the culture process have permeated the organization. Those responsible for cultural processes in particular are convinced that the formulation of a new, attractive target culture has led to a de facto change in the organization's actions. However, behind the scenes there are often complaints about the ineffectiveness of cultural projects and that the organization merely received a new coat of paint, without any change in everyday collaboration. Organizational consultant

Tom Peters, who in his early years was significantly involved in the discovery of culture under the name Thomas Peters, complained later on that in the "search for excellence" more than 90 percent of the money spent on cultural activities, in the form of training and counseling was wasted (cited in Bate 1997, 1049f.) What is this dissatisfaction with cultural programs linked with?

Ultimately, the cultural programs working with definitions such as "target cultures," with their harmonious and humanist prose, primarily affect the organization's display side. Now, we cannot underestimate the function of this display side for organizations. Every organization has to present a beautiful image to the outside world. Conflicting demands coming from the organization's environment must be at least partially satisfied by the presentation of lists of values that sound good. Internal conflicts must be concealed from the environment, because their discovery would lead to their further intensification. Within organizations, departments and hierarchical levels are also dependent on building up display sides. Departments present themselves to other departments as oriented towards the organizational goal, efficiently organized and largely free of conflict. Employees within the same hierarchy level also build up display sides to present to other hierarchy levels. We only need to look at how board members who are at odds with each other over technical questions try to present employees at lower hierarchy levels an image of harmony, or what efforts are made at lower hierarchy levels to conceal deviating objectives, padding and internal conflicts from board members.

Employees generally understand the vital necessity of "hypocrisy" of organizations in both their internal as external business

(Brunsson 1989). Employees at all levels of the hierarchy know very well that both the organization as a whole and individual departments have to "pretty up" in order to stand up well to the public, to retain qualified personnel on the labor market and to be perceived by other organizations as a respectable cooperation partner. However, cultural processes are not suitable for this kind of display side management, because they primarily have a claim to the inside and not the outside.

Employees have a fine sense for the differences between the catalogs of values presented on the display side and the culture that actually dominates the organization. Employees of a railway company recognize if a poster with a train running in a beautiful snow-covered landscape carries the slogan "Everybody talks about the weather, but we don't" but internally "spring, summer, autumn and winter" are referred to as the "four enemies of the railway company," because of the susceptibility of trains to weather. Employees pick up on the difference when a bank praises itself as "excellent" in its self-descriptions, even though a "culture of permanent complaints" has in fact developed behind the "facade of excellence" (Weeks 2004). And there will be consequences if the official cultural processes focus on the integrity of business practices, but all employees know that they are actually expected to bribe customers if it is the only way to win a contract.

In this respect, organizations react with cynicism to top-down organizational culture programs, which are presented to employees with appropriate behavioral requirements (Grey 2013, 69). When in a participatory process a supermarket chain points out that "customer focus" should be one of the organization's central values, the workers at the checkout do not smile at customers because they have internalized this value, but rather because they are aware of the surveillance cameras and the "mystery shoppers" sent to surreptitiously evaluate them (Ogbonna/Wilkinson 1990). If an attempt is made in a call center to combat the monotony of the activity by establishing an organizational culture of "playfulness" as in Internet startups, then this does not necessarily lead to a friendlier attitude towards customers. Employees experience a "fancy dress day" on which employees are supposed to dress up as "cheesy." Resentments against the imposition of a "culture of fun" lead to an even greater gulf opening up between employees and the company (Fleming 2005). Cultural programs of "imposed friendliness" and "forced playfulness" just lead employees to develop even more subtle mechanisms to show a "role distance" from activities they perceive to be stupid.

But this does not need to be a problem. Many organizations are able to put up with a high degree of cynicism. The main problem of these cultural processes, driven as they are by the fantasy to control, is that they coat the culture that actually exists in an organization. It is interesting to note that automobile companies carry out dozens of cultural processes without even one of them having gone into such depth that it would have been possible to discuss how different departments were able to meet the Board's ambitious targets for exhaust gas purification, mainly with creative interpretations of the law. It is striking that electronics companies, driven by waves of dismissals, have set up various programs to establish a culture of trust, without a single discussion of the fact that personal trust existed successfully even before the introduction of these cultural programs in those departments where bribes were systematically used to obtain contracts.

The claim that many cultural programs contribute to concealing the organizational culture may come as a surprise, since the aim of these programs is precisely the opposite, namely to uncover the existing organizational culture. But a glance at the typical tools offered for analyzing and changing cultures reveals how cultural programs conceal the actually existing culture.

A favorite instrument for surveying an organization's culture is working with metaphors. In workshops in the course of cultural audits, it is a frequent question which animal would characterize the organization best: an elephant, a good-natured animal which becomes aggressive when provoked; a crocodile lying apathetically in the river, but ruthlessly snapping when an opportunity presents itself? Or a hyena, which when hunting by its own is limited in its hunting possibilities, yet can bring down much bigger prey in cooperation with other hyenas? Or, in workshops, the employees are asked to imagine, under the guidance of cultural experts, what the organization would look like as a person: like a narcissistic 45-year-old man who is obsessed with himself and does not at all notice how everyone around him is turning away from him; like a tough, dynamic woman around the age of thirty, with whom everything fits on the outside, but who hides a deep sense of insecurity; or like an aging 60-year-old man who still dresses and acts like he was much younger? Or you can ask the participants of a workshop what kind of building best characterizes your own organization: for example, a "fortress" marked by security, a "theatre" marked by spectacle, or a "sanatorium" marked by a soothing climate.

These metaphors certainly have the charm that they are easily captured in organizational memory. People don't forget that their own organization was once described as a "hyena," an "old woman," or a "sanatorium." But it is precisely the use of such catchy metaphors that prevents the organization from delving into the details of specific practices. Precisely because they create associations to foreign contexts, metaphors quickly reach their limits when concretizing facts.

Another instrument is to shoehorn an organization's culture into a four-field scheme, which is particularly popular in business administration. Each of these four fields represents a possible cultural manifestation of an organization, which is described with one or two words. For example, an exaggerated "speculative culture" is contrasted with a short-term oriented "sales culture," a risk-oriented "investment culture" with a rigid "administrative culture" (Deal/Kennedy 1982). Or a "clan-like culture" created by the desire for consensus is put into relation to a dynamic "adhocratic culture," a formally oriented "hierarchical culture" or a "market-oriented culture" (Cameron/Quinn 1999). Or you can contrast a "market-oriented culture" oriented towards financial goals with a "bureaucratic culture," a "supported culture" characterized by shared values, with an "innovative culture" driven by experimentation. (Cardador/Rupp 2010). In the simpler variants of these four-field schemes, it is always clear that one of these four fields is better for the organization than all the others, while in the more intelligent variants it is emphasized that none of these cultures, which are reduced to one or two terms, is per se better than another, but that the organizations should pay attention to the "right fit" between their strategy and their culture. The charm of this definition of cultures on the base of four-field schemes is that consultants can quickly establish a quantitative determination of both an alleged "actual culture" and a "target culture" that can be visualized by questioning employees using standardized questionnaires. Such methods can be used with benefit if you want to start a discussion about values in the organization. But for the representation of cultural norms such thinking in two dimensions and four fields is not complex enough; indeed, due to the culmination into general values, the analysis of actual organizational-cultural norms tends to be ignored.

This obscuration of the de facto existing organizational culture is reinforced by the discrepancy analyses popular among cultural advisors (Sackmann 2006). These so-called "gap analyses" are about capturing the chasm between a current and a target status, in a quantitative manner. The data for this are either collected through a quantitative questioning of the employees about their perceived actual state and the desired target state, or by a survey of the actual state via observations of meetings, conferences and coffee breaks and of the target state via the analysis of mission statements, management principles, image brochures and annual reports. The results are then presented in spider diagrams showing the discrepancy between the actual state and the desired state. The results read like a wish list expressed in numbers, for more "open constructive communication," "learning orientation," "employee orientation," "granting freedom," "promotion of innovation," "customer orientation" and "sustainability orientation." However, the details of organizational-cultural expectations of behavior are not revealed.

> ### EXAMPLE
>
> ### An Example of Concealing an Organizational Culture by Means of a Cultural Program
>
> This is the story of a large U.S. electronics company that committed itself to cultural change with a "mea culpa program" after a particularly serious violation of the law. To move this change forward, cultural managers around the world were identified and sent on a journey to companies in Silicon Valley that were considered exemplary.
>
> While the parallel changes in the formal structure were mainly carried out by male employees —because those in exposed positions in production and assembly as well as in research and development were almost exclusively men—the cultural managers appointed by the division heads were almost exclusively women.
>
> This form of promotion of women in a very limited topic not only says a great deal about the organizational culture of the electronics company; the allocation of the "hard themes" to men and the "soft themes" to women was also an expression of how seriously top management took this cultural process. The "blind spot" created by the cultural process made it impossible to perceive this expression of contempt at all, let alone broach it.
>
> The cultural process always produced the same nice-sounding articulations of values: authenticity in communication, trust

> and sincerity in dealing with one another, reliable cooperation, objectivity in conflicts. Those in charge of culture were not even allowed to approach the culture that actually exists: the everyday practices in production and assembly and in research and development. (Smith 2015).

In order to avert a misunderstanding, we want to point out that a discussion of the organization's values using four-field schemes, analysis of the discrepancy between the target and actual culture, working with metaphors, and creating nice-sounding value catalogs can be helpful in many situations. This enables the creation of communicative catch-alls for upheavals in organizations, or a constantly necessary, largely inconsequential exchange can be made possible. However, we should not assume that those discussions bring any enlightenment about the culture that actually exists, let alone that they could be used to identify the starting points for a change of that culture.

3. Leverage for Influencing Organizational Culture

The fundamental problem of working on the organizational culture is that there is no certainty as to how employees will receive cultural programs. Organizational cultures develop as informal standards of action through repetition and imitation. And the norms of action, that are well established in this way, cannot be changed—this is the peculiarity of undecidable decision premises—by the proclamation of new cultural values. But what options are there then for management to influence the organizational culture?

The answer may seem paradoxical at first glance. The only tools that management holds for changing the organizational culture are changes in the formal structure. Not in the way that management with a passion for control might wish, namely, that the announcement of the formal structure might stimulate the appropriate changes in the organizational culture at the same time. Rather, this comes from the fact that any change in the official reporting channels, any proclamation of a new goal, any hiring, relocation or dismissal has an impact on how work is coordinated on an informal basis in the divisions, departments or teams.

For this reason, work on organizational culture must be carried out in a fundamentally different way than has been the case up to now. Since an organizational culture develops as a reaction to formal relationships, in an analysis phase the relationship between formality and informality in the organization must first be examined in detail. What are the prescribed communication channels, official programs and formalized expectations regarding personnel? How do they affect everyday work processes? Are there formal gaps in the rules that are filled by informal expectations? Are there sensible reasons for regular deviations from the organization's formal structure?

Some methods of organizational research are better than others for answering such questions. We know that quantitative surveys, conducted by means of standardized written or Internet-based surveys, tend to elicit answers that are socially desirable. Collecting such responses—as is also preferred in evidence-based management research—can make sense, for example, if you want to ascertain what the views of the management level are represented on the display side. They are unsuitable, however, for surveying expectations on the informal side because the details of organizational-cultural expectations cannot be assessed by standardized questionnaires and because respondents use the abstractness of the questionnaire to conceal everyday practices that deviate from the rules. Qualitative surveys conducted by means of participatory observations, observational interviews, individual interviews or group interviews, on the other hand, are much more suitable for assessing an organization's cultural expectations. Clearly, even when using these methods, the interviewees control the access to information about expectations and practices. Yet these survey methods make it considerably more difficult to hold back sensitive information.

The only way to obtain a complex understanding is through a combination of the various methods. Participatory observations—the more accurate term may be observatory participation—take place almost automatically whenever managers, consultants or scientists move around in the organization, lead meetings, and take part in discussions. The challenge is to maintain enough distance so that the informal expectations that seem so self-evident, so obvious, to everyone can still be recognized. In this regard, observational interviews are particularly helpful in the course of which people are asked about an activity while and after they are performing it. This enables a precise explanation of why production steps are exactly the way they are and not otherwise, why an observed police operation went so well, or why a file was processed in the observed way. Even if you don't have any qualms about dealing with the details of a production process, for example, you will be able to see why things are organized the way they are. One-on-one interviews represent a meaningful enhancement because they facilitate the development of a broader perspective. Various standard questions are appropriate at the beginning, such as, "Do you still remember your first day of work here? What surprised you? What did you expect to be different? What do you have to do here to gain good standing among your colleagues? How can you most easily turn colleagues against yourself? What do you have to do to gain the boss's respect? What do you have to do so it becomes impossible to work with you, or you even to get fired? What blunders should you avoid in particular? Are there colleagues who didn't make it past their trial period? Why did they leave the organization? Who is better off not applying for a job here? Why not? What would happen if they did?" The answers that come out of these standard questions make it possible to begin a detailed discussion of informal processes. Because group discussions, especially with members of organizations from different areas, can very quickly lead to the use of self-censorship mechanisms, they only make sense if there is a very good understanding of informal structures. Otherwise, there is a danger that you will only be fobbed off with abstract value formulations.

However, the subtleties of the organizational culture often only become clear once you try to influence it. To do this, you have to start directly with the formal structures: by changing the formal communication channels, the workflow processes and objectives, and the staffing of positions. It is never possible to predict exactly how such changes in formal structures will affect the behavior of employees. It is not uncommon for experienced managers and consultants to experience surprises about how changes in the formal structure affect the organizational culture. Organizational research, however, has produced reliable insights into the reactions that occur regularly at the informal level when the formal structure is changed.

3.1 Formalization of Programs, Communication Channels and Personnel as Leverage

One starting point for observing organizational culture is to focus on the informal evasive movements that develop in the individual types of organizational structure: programs, communication channels and personnel. In terms of their formal structure, organizations are a great puzzle in which work steps, communication channels and personnel decisions are precisely coordinated. But in the end, the big formal puzzle does not work in organizations. Instead, formal decisions about programs, communication channels and personnel lead to the emergence of informal compensation mechanisms. We can see this even at the level of the individual structural types.

We know from research on *programs* that rigid conditional programming through if-then rules is compensated for by informal evasive maneuvers. The routine work—regardless of whether we are talking about the assembly of engines in automobile production, the handling of calls in call centers, or visa issuance in embassies—is conditionally programmed in a formal way. If an engine part, a call or an application comes in, then it is dealt with in predefined steps. When there are unforeseen events or overloads, however, there is an informal expectation that employees in automobile factories, call centers and embassies will not adhere strictly to their conditional programs; instead, they informally take into account objectives such as time-sensitive order completion. Conversely, we also know that informal conditional programs also develop in consequence of the formal specification of goal programs with which the targets can be achieved or undermined, for example in the cases of sales targets for employees in pharmaceutical companies, publication targets for employees in research institutes, or the specification of the number of operations to be performed for doctors in hospitals. Formal decisions regarding one type of program often lead to reactions from another type of program, leading to adaptation processes at the informal level.

Informal compensations can also be observed in formally established *communication channels* that are symbolically represented by org charts in many organizations. The formal establishment of a functional organization—for example, the establishment of departments for purchasing, assembly, marketing and sales in a mechanical engineering company—means that regional aspects are not particularly taken into account. Since the formal elements can only address regional problems to a limited extent, informal mechanisms for exchanging information on regional issues arise. Or, in another example, the establishment of largely autonomous business units as the formal basic structure of a corporate group necessarily leads to competition between these units. Just as there is a basic attitude in automobile factories that the main competitors are not the other automobile companies, but the other factories within their own corporation, there is a saying in armies of different countries that the army's greatest enemies are their own air force and navy. Competition for resources within an organization seems to be more important for the survival of sub-organizations than competition with other organizations. To understand organizational culture, it is not just these competitive relationships—often concealed by harmonious mission statements on the display side—that are relevant, but also the informal balancing mechanisms with which the autonomous sub-organizations try to uphold cooperation at certain points, despite a formal structure designed for competition. Regardless of whether organizations, or units of organizations, formally give themselves a functional, regional, center or matrix structure: in all cases there can be observed compensation mechanisms in their organizational culture.

We also see organizational-cultural compensation mechanisms when it comes to aspects of *personnel*. Many organizations view the selection of personnel as an opportunity to exercise influence on decisions. Large companies that see themselves as crusty or old-fashioned hope to change their attitude, and thus also their decisions, by recruiting employees from hip start-ups, promoting "young guns," dismissing older employees under the guise of premature retirement, and waging colorful personnel development campaigns labeled on "cultural change." This indeed affects in parts the level of formal structure, but the reactions in the organizational culture are more interesting. Informal evasion and compensation maneuvers are at least as relevant, for example in the form of superficial adaptation to the "new way of thinking," the retreat into a camp of custodians of traditional values, or the emergence of "complaint corners" where people make fun of ingratiation to start-ups, the young guns, or hip cultural programs.

In short, changing formal structures always result in a reaction on the informal side. This can be an informal addition to the formal structure, which has the function of compensating for control gaps. However, it can also be an informal counter-structure that offsets, by selectively breaking the rules, the rigidities of formal expectation.

3.2 Abandonment of Formalization as a Strategy for Changing Organizational Culture

A second approach to influencing organizational culture is to reduce the degree of formalization in an organization. The reasons for this can widely vary: frustration at too much bureaucracy in an organization; adaptations to the management modes of de-formalization that are propagated under ultimately interchangeable concepts such as adhocratism, sociocracy, holacracy or agilocracy; or the profound conviction that democracy is not only suitable for the governance of states, but also of companies, administrations, police forces and armies. Interestingly, when organizations abandon formalization, this does not create a culture of "anything goes"; instead, a new culture arises, one that consists of tried and tested routines, well-established patterns of cooperation and resilient networks of people.

In *programs*, de-formalization consists not of prescribing processes and goals from the top and in detail, but rather of relying on the development of tried and tested routines and meaningful goals throughout the everyday practice. Processes in the form of conditional programs emerge slowly; they are not formally prescribed by management. Goals are defined jointly, not by top management, yet they can be missed, modified or abandoned, without violating the membership rules. The ability of organizations to develop informal routines and goals in the absence of formal guidelines is considerable. However, experience has shown that demands for standardization of routines and better coordination of goals come about quickly, and this ultimately means nothing less than a stronger formalization of the organizational structure.

According to the advocates of de-formalization, the official *communication channels*—especially the hierarchical ones—should be as weak as possible. Certainly, people are looking for formal alternatives to the classical hierarchy, for example in the form of voting in assemblies, the establishment of bodies committed to the principle of consensus, or the election of superiors by subordinates. Ultimately, however, the ideal concept is that of an all-channel network in which everyone can communicate with each other (Bavelas 1949). Thanks to research on organizations without formal hierarchies—political grass-roots groups, self-governed enterprises and anarchist terrorist organizations— we know which organizational-cultural reaction patterns form when organizations largely renounce formal hierarchies (it is still worthwhile in this regard to read Michels 1911). Informal hierarchies form within organizations because individuals will assume leadership roles in critical situations. Instead of a formal order of precedence that is issued from above and binding for all, there is an informal ranking. This can be functional, especially for organizations that rely on a high degree of identification with their purpose, because the people who assume leadership roles depend on the support, or at least toleration, of everyone else and thus an alienation from the organization is reduced. At the same time, such organizations also face difficulties because of their culture. For example, they can only react slowly to unforeseen events because, for reasons of internal legitimacy, everyone has to be included. This means there is a comparatively strong reservoir of perseverance because a broad consensus always has to be established, and problems arise because external cooperation partners have difficulties in finding a responsible contact person who can also enforce agreements in their organization.

When it comes to decision on *personnel*, organizations can elect to largely dispense with formalization. Hardly any formal criteria are laid down for recruitment, transfer, dismissal and staff development, and instead there is a reliance on mechanisms for regulating membership to emerge out of everyday practice. Entry into such organizations often takes place through one's own network of acquaintances, which can promote the already existing "good personal relationships." Particularly in organizations that try to do away with formalized processes, we predominantly find fluid boundaries between personal and organizational relationships, between leisure and work and—if enough erotic tension has been built up—also between family and organization. De-formalization advocates imagine that the assumption of new tasks does not take place through formal promotions, but rather through the fact that employees declare themselves responsible for it; sometimes, this leads to a problematic situation in which several people declare themselves responsible in competition with each other. For supporters of de-formalization, personnel development planned from above and focusing on the education of employees tends to be the exception. Instead, their aim is to ensure that employees are successfully socialized into the organization. Terminations can then only be enforced by the formal membership rules in a very limited way since those rules only exist to a limited extent. Instead, such firings—as we know from research on political organizations—often take place through the more or less socially tolerable method of being driven off by other members of the organization (Freeman 1972, 160).

In brief, there can be good reasons for organizations to largely dispense with the formalization of expectations. However, the culture that develops in informality in response to this renunciation of formalization has nothing to do with the organizational paradise promised by the advocates of new management fashions, in prose teeming with buzzwords such as trust, esteem and respect. "No structure," the organizational scholar Henry Mintzberg observed (Mintzberg 1979, 462), "is more Darwinian, none promotes more the fit—as long as they remain fit—and none is more devastating for the weak, than a structure that largely renounces formalization. The French have an evocative description of an organizational culture produced by eschewing formalization, which is often characterized by mighty power struggles: *un panier du crabes*, or a basket full of crabs; they are all pinching each other to work their way up higher, or even to get out."

3.3 Increased Formalization as a Starting Point for Shaping the Organizational Culture

A third approach is to formalize as many expectations as possible in the organization; i.e., to make the fulfillment of such expectations into an enforceable and controllable condition for membership. The reasons for such an increased formalization of expectations can vary widely. Top management may fear a loss of control and react with a formalization campaign. Often, however, formalization is also demanded "from the bottom up" because employees demand "more orientation" or "more security." Sometimes rationalization measures are also considered the starting point of formalizations because it is hoped that further regulation will reduce the "slack," or the organization's "padding." Another reason for increased formalization may be legal requirements for the precise documentation of work processes, or the hope of being able to assign responsibilities to individual persons at any time within a very deep hierarchy.

Increased formalization of *programs* can be based both on if-then rules (the conditional programs) and on objectives (the goal programs). The first starting point is to use if-then rules to more precisely specify the actions of employees. This is expressed by the fact that workflows are further detailed in process manuals and software programs. A few examples of such formalization in the form of if-then rules are the rules and regulations of administrations for processing applications for passports, building permits or welfare assistance; the process manuals of fast food chains for servicing customers; or the software-controlled specifications for speech sequences for call center employees. The second starting point for the formalization of membership conditions is a highly differentiated specification of objectives. Organizational members are given very detailed instructions on which "smart goals"—meaning targets that are specific, measurable, appealing, realistic and scheduled (Doran 1981)—have to be achieved. Typical examples of such formalization strategies are the detailed specification of sales targets for sales personnel or production specifications for assembly teams. Such measures have the effect that, although organization members generally orient themselves towards the formal requirements, they are forced again and again to deviate from this detailed set of rules. The more precisely an organization specifies its formal programs, the more difficult it is to adapt to changing requirements.

An increased formalization of *communication channels* means a tightening of the rules about who is allowed to speak to whom, and when, in an organization. As a rule, care is taken to ensure that the hierarchical communication channels are precisely described, coordination with other departments takes place via narrowly defined channels, and contacts with other organizations are only carried out via designated interface points. However, we also see informal evasive movements here. In order to be able to react quickly, accelerated informal communication channels develop across the hierarchy levels, coordination procedures between departments are established despite being actually prohibited, and informal interface points through which other organizations can establish contacts are built up.

Organizations can also rely on increased formalization in the structural component of *personnel*. This means that the requirements profile is formally and precisely defined prior to the recruitment of new personnel, and larger selection committees can be set up to avoid arbitrariness in recruitment process. Requirements can be specified for a career in the organization, for example, that employees must have passed an assessment test by HR before they can climb to the next level. Formal criteria can also be laid down for large waves of redundancies, specifying that it is primarily employees with the shortest length of service who will be dismissed. However, the strong formalization of decisions on recruitment, promotion and dismissal also causes informal evasions (Frost et al. 1985). It is well known that critical recruitment efforts do not go to the one who most closely fulfills the formal criteria, but rather to the candidate who is presumed to fit best into the social structure; that senior executives are able to push through the promotion of former personal assistants, even if they have failed the prescribed assessment test; or that employees with a brief term of service can also survive a wave of redundancies if those responsible in the company know that their expertise is important for the organization.

In brief, there may be good reasons for an increased formalization of behavioral expectations in organizations. But informal evasions will be an inevitable response to formalization, with the exception of organizations or divisions that operate in very stable environments. Some of these informal evasions will move in the grey area of what is just formally acceptable, while others will violate the formal order. Because contradictory requirements cannot be squeezed into a consistent formal system of rules, increased formalization ultimately leads to an increase in rule violations at the level of the organizational culture.

4. Conclusion—
Consequences for Influencing Organizational Cultures

For practitioners, it is inevitably frustrating that any decision to change the formal structures entails not only anticipated and desired, but also unwanted, side effects on the organizational culture side. But that's what organizational research has taught us about organizations. There is no optimal organizational structure that satisfies everyone and everything. Every decision always brings surprises, disappointments and problems. Those who are not prepared to live with this fact should stay away from companies, administrations, armies, universities, schools, political parties and associations.

Clearly, you can put together an imaginary dream world for the organization that consists of values such as trust, esteem, respect, authenticity, loyalty and creativity. But it is no coincidence that these organizational promises of salvation come either from individual consultants, coaches or management gurus, all of whom have very good reasons to no longer want to deal with an organization on a day-to-day basis as an employed member; from members of mini-organizations who believe that the behaviors in their micro-organizations with five or six members can be freely scaled for large organizations; or from persons at the top of the organization who almost always have a more positive image of their organization than their employees do.

But the observation that changes in the formal structure lead to unwanted side effects in the organizational culture must not be understood as a plea for a completely laissez-faire, "anything goes" attitude. On the contrary: it is precisely because changes in the formal structure always entail changes in the organizational culture that it is important to anticipate these as well as possible. The modification of the formal structures should be carried out with a kind of "risk management" that tries to account for the resulting changes in the informal structures. In other words, in any change process you have to avoid concentrating on only one side of the organization.

Concerning projects for the design of organizations one can observe that they often only focus on one side of the organization. On the display side, PR agencies, advertising companies or marketing experts are hired to set up, maintain and, if necessary, repair the facade of the organization. For the formal side, the world's classic expert consulting firms are called in. They are expected to "reengineer" the organization's formal processes, to make the organizational chart "leaner" by dissolving departments or hierarchical levels, or to "redesign" the formal assignment of employees. For the organizational climate and culture—the informal side— the "culture specialists" are then called upon in the form of the systemic process consultants, trainers or coaches who are supposed to ensure that the interpersonal "chemistry," or the informal coordination apart from the formal specifications, between the employees is correct.

These specialists for the different sides of the organization have their own blind spots. The specialists for the display side can, to a large extent, beautify the facade of the organization without having to worry about what implications this external image has on the inside. The formal side specialists—whether they are experts in strategic realignment, increasing efficiency or improving quality processes—tend to place exaggerated hopes in the formalization of organizations. The management announces strategic reorientations, calculates efficiency gains by changing the formal structure, or declares that the formal quality standards are now fully adhered to, without noticing that completely different structures have already developed on the informal side. The specialists for the informal side, who are often called upon to deal with these unintended side effects of the reorganizations, may sometimes identify aspects of the formal structure as reasons for the deterioration of things, but they rarely have the competence to fundamentally spearhead these reorganizations (Scott-Morgan 1994).

EXAMPLE

Example: Cultural Programs and the Taboo on Discussing the Effects of a Reorganization Project

A large U.S. private bank has been discussing its organizational structure for some time now. In the team responsible for complex loans, the very good employees are not only responsible for identifying interesting projects, but also for handling the rather simple contract processing and accompanying the projects after the conclusion of the contract. This has the positive effect that the project managers have good detailed insights into these often very complex projects, even after the contract has been closed and can thus learn for future loan projects. At the same time, however, it is becoming increasingly clear that the highly paid project employees spend a lot of time on the rather monotonous business of contract processing and that expertise on the contractual, tender and lending processes is concentrated nowhere else in the bank.

As part of a major reorganization project, the new CEO engages a globally active expert consulting firm, for which she used to work as a consultant in the past, in order to analyze and standardize the processes. The consulting firm suggests that the responsibility for contracts, grants and loans should be separated from the teams responsible for projects and these tasks should be concentrated in dedicated contract teams. The aim of the project is to bundle competences into teams and thus, as is customary in the banking industry, define clear responsibilities for the market, back office and credit service, bundle competences for contract processing and save personnel costs by employing lower paid employees in the newly formed contract teams.

But only a few months after the end of the project, severe distortions become apparent. The newly created teams for contract management do not cooperate well with the teams responsible for project acquisition. The poorer pay of some employees leads to a "two-class society," which makes cooperation across team boundaries difficult. There are coordination problems at the interfaces between the teams, creating annoying delays for the customers when concluding the contract. It is becoming increasingly clear that the reorganization, contrary to the consultants' promises, has slowed down processes and made them more expensive.

Although the unintended side effects of the reorganization became clear very quickly, a withdrawal of the measure is taboo. The CEO has put her neck on the line with the project vis-à-vis the Supervisory Board, the reorganization project has cost the bank a double-digit million sum, and the employees are only just now beginning to "recover" from the unrest caused by the reorganization. Therefore, the reorganization must not be discussed as the cause of the current problems under any circumstances. Instead, people identify the absence of a "culture of cooperation" in the bank, which is to be addressed by means of an isolated program.

For this purpose, "cultural specialists" are engaged to develop joint guiding principles for the bank. These guiding principles, which were developed in a project group and approved by the Executive Board, call for "more courage for a straightforward division of labor between the teams," "more concentration on communication between the teams" and "faster and more authentic stimuli from the managers." In a broad rollout, these guidelines are communicated to employees who are asked to reflect on what these guidelines mean for the collaboration of specialized teams.

Doing things this way allows the board of directors to send a signal to the employees that they have noticed the deterioration in the working atmosphere, yet without needing to put hands on the "holy reorganization." At the same time, however, it also became clear that the guidelines did not fundamentally change the problems created by the reorganization. On the contrary, the employees recognize that the process in the guiding principles is a measure to pass the responsibilities for a reorganization on them that they consider to be unsuccessful. Sarcasm increases among bank employees, even though the bank has, thus far, been free of cynicism (Smith 2015).

As a rule, specialists do not have to pay much attention to the effects that their actions have on other sides of the organization. The specialists for the display side praise the improved external presentation, but rarely have to justify themselves for the reaction of the employees to the changed display side years later. The assignment to formal-side specialists to revise the organizational charts, to change the process manuals and to reassign staff is usually forgotten when the undesired effects of the reorganization become clear, especially in the case of informal side effects. By concentrating on accepted value formulations, the specialists for organizational culture quickly succeed in establishing consensus; however, they do not have to justify themselves for how the commitment to the values formulated by them has had an effect in practice, even more so since the damage caused by the informal effects cannot be quantified.

In spite of all the understanding for the advantages of division of labor, organizations do themselves no favor if they focus their change projects on only one side of the organization. Projects that try to enhance the display side of the organization through the formulation of mission statements often lead to cynicism among employees, unless they are systematically connected to the formal and informal side. Projects on the formal side of the organization, which do not systematically reflect the effects on the display side and the informal side, may be presented as a success in the short term, but they often turn out to be "change ruins" later on. And organizational culture projects have, at best, a cosmetic effect if the formal structure is not systematically questioned. Eventually, such projects do not lead to fundamental changes in the organization.

The three sides of the organization—the display side, the formal side and the informal side— have different functions, but in change processes initiated by management, one must always keep an eye on all three sides. If managers who engage renowned consulting firms—which are committed to transforming organizational charts, redesigning processes or redeploying personnel with the promise of strategic realignment or efficiency improvement—do not precisely reflect on the informal reactions to these changes, you can bet that they will experience "cultural surprises" down the road and will feel the tendency to create programs that will "fix" the culture. If the management has set up a process for shaping organizational culture and thereby explicitly or implicitly communicates that the formal structure must not be touched, it can be assumed from the outset that this process will remain largely ineffective.

At first glance, this seems like a plea against programs for the design of organizational culture. But ultimately, there is no reason not to create programs under the title of organizational culture if they are used as a kind of "Trojan horse" to work on the prescribed communication channels, formal programs and official policies in the field of personnel. After all, changing these is the only effective way to influence organizational culture.

Bibliography

Alvesson, Mats. 2013. *Understanding Organizational Culture*. 2nd ed. London: Sage.

Bardmann, Theodor M., and Reiner Franzpötter. 1990. "Unternehmenskultur: Ein postmodernes Organisationskonzept." *Soziale Welt* 41: 424–40.

Bate, S. P. 1997. "Whatever Happened to Organizational Anthropology? A Review of the Field of Organizational Ethnography and Anthropological Studies." *Human Relations* 50: 1147–75.

Bavelas, Alex. 1949. *Some Effects of Certain Communication Patterns Upon Group Performance*. Boston: Massachusetts Institute of Technology.

Bleicher, Knut. 1986. "Strukturen und Kulturen der Organisation im Umbruch: Herausforderungen für den Organisator." *Zeitschrift Führung & Organisation* 2: 97–106.

Brunsson, Nils. 1989. *The Organization of Hypocrisy: Talk, Decisions and Actions in Organizations*. Chichester et al.: John Wiley & Sons.

Cameron, Kim S., and Robert E. Quinn. 1999. *Diagnosing and Changing Organizational Culture*. Reading: Addison-Wesley.

Cardador, Teresa M., and Deborah E. Rupp. 2010. "Organizational Culture, Multiple Needs, and the Meaningfulness of Work." In *The Handbook of Organizational Culture and Climate*. 2nd ed., 158–80. London: Sage.

Carleton, J. R., and Claude S. Lineberry. 2010. *Achieving Post-Merger Success: A Stakeholder's Guide to Cultural Due Diligence, Assessment, and Integration.* San Francisco: Pfeiffer.

Connors, Roger, and Tom Smith. 2012. *Change the Culture, Change the Game: The Breakthrough Strategy for Energizing your Organization and Creating Accountability for Results.* London: Portfolio/Penguin.

Deal, Terrence E., and Allan A. Kennedy. 1982. *Corporate Cultures: The Rites and Rituals of Corporate Life.* Reading: Addison-Wesley.

Deetz, Stanley A., Sarah J. Tracy, and Jennifer L. Simpson. 2000. *Leading Organizations Through Transition: Communication and Cultural Change.* Thousand Oaks/London/New Delhi: Sage.

Doppler, Klaus, and Christoph Lauterburg. 2002. *Change Management: Den Unternehmenswandel gestalten.* 10th ed. Frankfurt a.M./New York: Campus.

Doran, George T. 1981. "There's a S.M.a.R.T. Way to Write Management's Goals and Objectives." *Management Review* 70: 35–36.

Drucker, Peter F. 1954. *The Practice of Management.* New York: Harper & Row.

Fleming, Peter. 2005. "'Workers' Playtime: Boundaries and Cynicism in a 'Culture of Fun' Program." *Journal of Applied Behavioral Science* 41: 285–303.

Foster, Richard, and Sarah Kaplan. 2001. *Creative Destruction: Why Companies That Are Built to Last Underperform the Market and How to Successfully Transform Them.* New York: Crown Business.

Freeman, Jo. 1972. "The Tyranny of Structurelessness." *Berkeley Journal of Sociology* 17: 151–64.

Frost, Peter J., Larry F. Moore, Meryl R. Louis, Craig C. Lundberg, and Joanne Martin. 1985. "An Allegorical View of Organizational Culture." In *Organizational Culture*, edited by Peter J. Frost, Larry F. Moore, Meryl R. Louis, Craig C. Lundberg, and Joanne Martin, 13-25. Beverly Hills/London: Sage.

Gagliardi, Pasquale. 1986. "The Creation and Change of Organizational Cultures: A Conceptual Framework." *Organizational Studies* 7: 117–34.

Goffman, Erving. 1967. "The Nature of Deference and Demeanor." In *Interaction Ritual: Essays in Face-to-Face Behaviour*, edited by Erving Goffman, 47–96. New York/London: Allen Lane Penguin.

Grey, Christopher. 2013. *A Very Short, Fairly Interesting and Reasonably Cheap Book About Studying Organizations.* 3rd ed. London/Thousand Oaks/New Delhi/Singapore: Sage.

Hofstede, Geert. 1980. *Culture's Consequences: International Differences in Work Related Values.* Beverly Hills, London: Sage.

Huntington, Samuel P. 1968. *Political Order in Changing Societies.* New Haven/London: Yale University Press.

Klimecki, Rüdiger, Gilbert Probst, and Peter Eberl. 1994. *Entwicklungsorientiertes Management.* Stuttgart: Schäffer-Poeschel.

Kobi, Jean-Marcel, and Hans A. Wüthrich. 1986. *Unternehmenskultur verstehen, erfassen und gestalten.* Landsberg: Verlag Moderne Industrie.

Krackhardt, David, and Jeffrey R. Hanson. 1993. "Informal Networks: The Company Behind the Chart." *Harvard Business Review* 71 (4): 104–13.

Kühl, Stefan. 2013. *Organizations: A Systems Approach.* Farnham: Gower.

Kühl, Stefan. 2016. *Ordinary Organizations: Why Normal Men Carried out the Holocaust.* Cambridge/Malden: Polity Press.

Kühl, Stefan. 2017. *Developing Strategies: A Very Brief Introduction.* Princeton/Hamburg/Shanghai/Singapore/Versailles/Zurich: Organizational Dialogue Press.

Kühl, Stefan. 2018 (forthcoming). *Sisyphus in Management: The Futile Search for the Optimal Organizational Structure.* Princeton/Hamburg/Shanghai/Singapore/Versailles/Zurich: Organizational Dialogue Press.

Lorsch, Jay W. 1986. "Managing Culture: The Invisible Barrier to Strategic Change." *California Management Review* 28: 95–109.

Luhmann, Niklas. 1964. *Funktionen und Folgen formaler Organisation.* Berlin: Duncker & Humblot.

Luhmann, Niklas. 1970. *Allgemeines Modell organisierter Sozialsysteme.* Bielefeld: Unpublished manuscript.

Luhmann, Niklas. 1971. "Reform des öffentlichen Dienstes." In *Politische Planung*, edited by Niklas Luhmann, 203–56. Opladen: WDV.

Luhmann, Niklas. 1972. *Rechtssoziologie.* Reinbek: Rowohlt.

Luhmann, Niklas. 1984. *Soziale Systeme: Grundriß einer allgemeinen Theorie.* Frankfurt a.M.: Suhrkamp.

Luhmann, Niklas. 2000. *Organisation und Entscheidung.* Opladen: WDV.

Mann, Leon. 1969. "Queue Culture: The Waiting Line as a Social System." *American Journal of Sociology* 75: 340–54.

Marshall, Judie, and Adrian Mclean. 1985. "Exploring Organisation Culture as a Route to Organisational Change." In *Current*

Research in Management, edited by Valerie Hammond, 2–20. London: Francis Pinter.

Maslow, Abraham H. 1954. *Motivation and Personality.* New York: Harper.

Mayo, Elton. 1948. *The Human Problems of an Industrial Civilization*. New York: Macmillan.

Michels, Robert. 1911. *Zur Soziologie des Parteiwesens in der modernen Demokratie: Untersuchungen über die oligarchischen Tendenzen des Gruppenlebens.* Leipzig: Verlag von Dr. Werner Klinkhardt.

Mintzberg, Henry. 1979. *The Structuring of Organizations: A Synthesis of the Research.* Englewood Cliffs: Prentice-Hall.

Morgan, Gareth. 1986. *Images of Organization.* Beverly Hills: Sage.

Ogbonna, Emmanuel, and Barry Wilkinson. 1990. "Corporate Strategy and Corporate Culture: The View from the Checkout." *Personnel Review* 19: 9–15.

Ouchi, William G. 1981. *Theory Z: How American Business Can Meet the Japanese Challenge.* New York: Addison Wesley.

Peters, Thomas J., and Robert H. Waterman. 1982. *In Search of Excellence.* New York: Harper & Row.

Rodríguez Mansilla, Darío. 1991. *Gestion organizacional: Elementos para su estudio.* Santiago de Chile: Pontificia Universidad Católica de Chile.

Rodríguez Mansilla, Darío. 2004. *Diagnóstico organizacional.* 6th ed. Santiago de Chile: Ediciones Universidad Católica de Chile.

Roethlisberger, Fritz J., and William J. Dickson. 1939. *Management and the Worker: An Account of a Research Program*

Conducted by the Western Electric Company, Hawthorne Works, Chicago. Cambridge: Harvard University Press.

Rottenburg, Richard. 1996. "When Organization Travels: On Intercultural Translation." In *Translating Organizational Change*, edited by Czarniawska, Barbara, and Guje Sevón, 191–240. Berlin/New York: Walter de Gruyter.

Sackmann, Sonja A. 1991. *Cultural Knowledge in Organizations.* Newbury Park: Sage.

Sackmann, Sonja A. 2006. *Success Factor: Corporate Culture: Developing a Corporate Culture for High Performance and Long-Term Competitveness.* Gütersloh: Verlag Bertelsmann Stiftung.

Schein, Edgar H. 1985. *Organizational Culture and Leadership.* London: Jossey-Bass.

Schein, Edgar H.. 1996. "Culture: The Missing Concept in Organization Studies." *Administrative Science Quarterly* 41: 229–40.

Schein, Edgar H.. 1999. *The Corporate Culture Survival Guide.* San Francisco: Jossey-Bass.

Schnyder, Alphons B. 1992. "Die Entwicklung zur Innovationskultur." *Organisationsentwicklung* (1): 62–69.

Scott-Morgan, Peter. 1994. *The Unwritten Rules of the Game: Master Them, Shatter Them, and Break Through the Barriers to Organizational Change.* New York: McGraw-Hill.

Smith, Rebecca. 2015. *Organizational Culture: Case Studies.* Princeton: Unpublished manuscript.

Solomon, Cynthia. 2004. *Culture Audits: Supporting Organizational Success.* Alexandria: ASTD.

Taylor, Carolyn. 2015. *Walking the Talk: Building a Culture for Success.* Revised edition. London: Random House Business Books.

Weeks, John. 2004. *Unpopular Culture: The Ritual of Complaint in a British Bank.* Chicago: University of Chicago Press.

Weick, Karl E. 1995. *Sensemaking in Organizations.* Thousand Oaks/London/New Delhi: Sage.

Young, Ed. 1989. "On the Naming of the Rose: Interests and Multiple Meanings as Elements of Organizational Culture." *Organization Studies* 10 (2): 187–206.

www.ingramcontent.com/pod-product-compliance
Lightning Source LLC
Chambersburg PA
CBHW020302030426
42336CB00010B/877